Discovery 4

Pupil's Book

written by
Melanie Behrendt
Nadine Gulden
Kirstin Jebautzke

advised by
Bettina Attig
Isabella Bach
Diana Hein
Elbie Picker
Ina Schroeder

illustrated by
Carmen Hochmann, Falko Honnen,
Markus Humbach, Theresia Koppers,
Isabelle Metzen, Katja Rau,
Friederike Schumann

westermann

Contents

Welcome back

CD 1 **1 Listen and point.**

2 Talk about your holidays.

In town

STATION
TOWN HALL
Vampire's night
Whales
Love forever
CINEMA
CASTLE
HOSPITAL
HUNGRY EYE
BAKERY
TAXI
MH1 ABK
Bus Stop
12
23
STATION
23

Lucy lives in Windsor.
Windsor is an old English town.
There are many shops and restaurants,
a church and a castle.
The big building with the flag
is the town hall.
Can you see Lucy?
She is on her way to the cinema.

CD 7
CD 8

1 Listen and point.

2 Talk to a partner:
Where's …?
– The … is next to …

3 Read the text.

Kinder anregen, ihr Wissen zum Thema einzubringen · Bildbeschreibung hören und auf Bildausschnitte zeigen · Einzelheiten des Bildes benennen / beschreiben · Fragen zum Bild beantworten, z. B. *Where's …?/Can you find …?* · Text lesen

Flashcards
Poster

Map of Windsor

CD 10 **1 Listen and point.**

2 Work with a partner: *Where's the hospital? – It's in A2.*

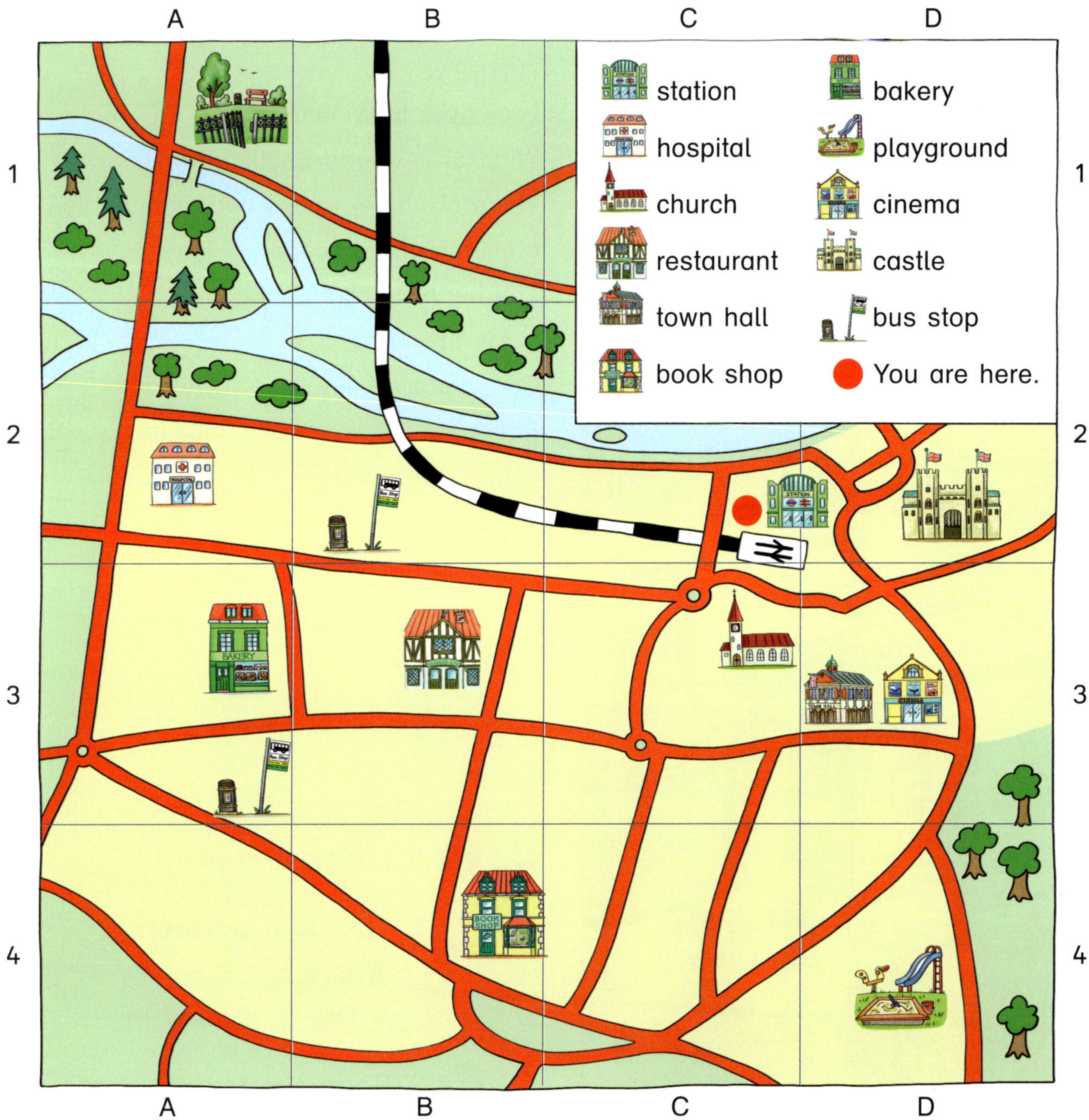

Hörtext hören, entsprechende Gebäude auf der Karte finden · in Partnerarbeit Lage von Gebäuden erfragen · **D↑** Rätsel formulieren: *It's in B 2. It's next to the station. What is it?*

AB S. 4
Copy 2 – 5
Flashcards

Finding the way

CD 11 **1 Listen and read.**

2 Create a new dialogue.

Tourist: Excuse me.
Can you help me, please?
How do I get to the cinema?
Policeman: Well, let's see.
We are in front of the station.
Go straight on, then turn left at the church.
Walk down the street.
Then turn right.
You'll see the cinema.
It's on your right.
Tourist: Thank you very much.
Policeman: You're welcome.

Turn left. Go straight on. Turn right.

3 Work with a partner.

CD 9 **4 Say the rap.**

Dialog hören und mitlesen · veränderten Dialog mit einem Partner sprechen · D veränderten Dialog schreiben · Sprachmuster in Dialog anwenden · D *How do I get from ... to ...?* · Rap *Can you tell me the way?* hören, sprechen und sich entsprechend bewegen

AB S. 5
Copy 6/7

Going to the cinema

CD 14 **1 Listen and read.**

Geschichte hören und mitlesen · Fragen zur Geschichte beantworten ·
D⬆ Inhalt der Geschichte auf Englisch wiedergeben

AB S. 6/7
Copy 8/9
Copy 10/11

At the cinema

CD 15 **1 Listen and read.**

2 Read out loud.

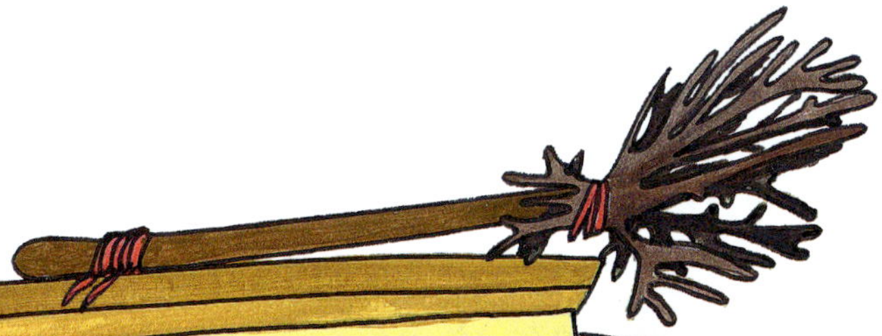

The forgetful witch

The old witch was getting ready
for a witch party.
It was already quarter to twelve
and she couldn't find her shoes.
"Have you seen my shoes?"
she asked her black cat.
"Oh, you are so forgetful.
They are under your bed," her cat said.
"And where is my hat?
Have you seen my hat?"
she asked her black cat.
"Oh, you are so forgetful," her cat said.
"It's on the wardrobe."
"And where is my broom?
Have you seen my broom?"
the old witch asked her black cat.
"Oh, you are so forgetful," her cat said.
"Why don't you use magic to find
your shoes, the hat and the broom?"
"Good idea, Cat," said the old witch.
"But – have you seen my magic wand?"

3 Work with a partner: *Which film would you like to see?*
– I'd like to see ...

Kinder anregen, über ihre Kinoerfahrungen zu berichten · Texte hören und mitlesen · Fragen zur Geschichte beantworten · ggf. Inhalt auf Deutsch zusammenfassen (Sprachmittlung) · Text mit verteilten Rollen lesen · D ⬆ Text als Rollenspiel umsetzen und vorspielen

AB S. 8

Animals in town

CD 16 **1 Listen and point.**

2 Talk to a partner: *Where's the ...? – It's in/on/behind/next to ...*

Text hören und auf entsprechenden Bildausschnitt zeigen · Fragen zum Text beantworten · mit einem Partner darüber sprechen, wo sich die Tiere im Bild befinden: *The squirrel is ...* · D ↑ sich im Internet/in Fachbüchern über *Animals in town* informieren

AB S. 9
Copy 12/13
Flashcards

In a dark, dark park

CD 17 1 Listen and read along.

2 D⬆ Read out loud.

It was a dark, dark night.
In the dark, dark town
there was a dark, dark park.
And in the dark, dark park
there was a dark, dark tree.
And in the dark, dark tree
there was a dark, dark hole.
And in the dark, dark hole
there was a dark, dark nest.
And in the dark, dark nest
there was a dark, dark owl.
And under the dark, dark owl
there was ...

Look around: Shopping

CD 18 **1 Listen and point.**

at the market

in the shopping centre

in the book shop

in the post office

at the supermarket

at the corner shop

2 D⬆ Do a roleplay.

Eindruck von Einkaufsmöglichkeiten in Großbritannien bekommen · Unterschiede und Gemeinsamkeiten im deutschen und britischen Stadtleben feststellen · äußern, wo man gern etwas einkaufen würde · Dialoge hören und den Einkaufslokalitäten zuordnen · D⬆ Einkaufsdialoge nachsprechen

Discovery tour

Can you find it?

Rocket game

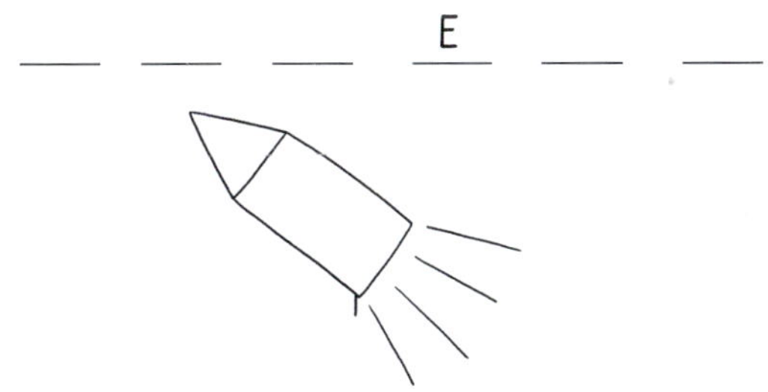

Listen and say

There are many bees
in the green trees.
How many can you see?

CD 19

Tounge twister

Three witches watch three watches.
Which witch watches which watch?

CD 20

People at work

The children are talking about their jobs.
Today there is a guest in Lucy's class.
Collin the cook is telling them about his job.
The children are very interested.
They're helping Collin to make sandwich faces.
There are also jobs to do in the classroom.
This week Kamal and Harry have to sweep the floor.
Amy and Tom have to clean the blackboard.
Have you got jobs to do in your class?

CD 24 **1 Listen and point.**

2 Talk to a partner:
What do you like on your sandwich? – I like …

3 Read the text.

What's your job?

CD 25
CD 26

1 Listen and point.

Peter is a postman.

Bob is a bus driver.

Tina is a teacher.

Sheldon is a shop assistant.

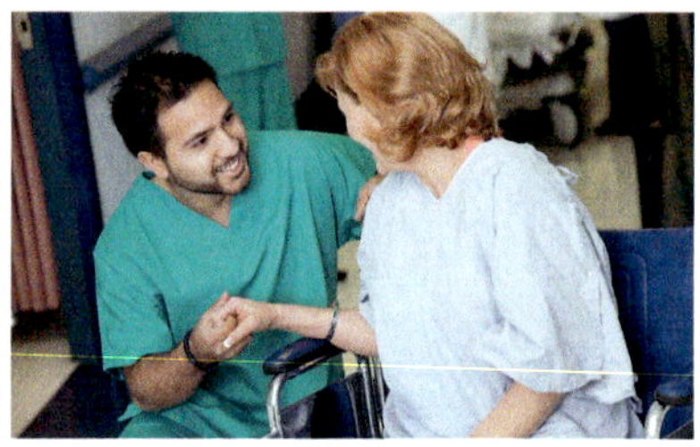

Norman is a nurse.

Diana is a doctor.

CD 27

2 Listen and read.

3 Act out your own interview.

Lucy: What's your name?

Mike: My name is Mike.

Lucy: What's your job?

Mike: I'm a mechanic.

Lucy: When do you start work?

Mike: At seven in the morning.

Lucy: When do you finish?

Mike: Usually at four in the afternoon.

Lucy: Do you like your job?

Mike: Yes, I do.

Text hören, Geräusche hören, auf entsprechende Bilder zeigen, Sätze lesen, Gleichklang der Anfangsbuchstaben erkennen · Interview mit verteilten Rollen lesen · D↑ Rollenspiel

Copy 16/17/18
AB S. 12/13
Flashcards

Job song

CD 29
CD 30

1 Listen and sing along.

1 Toby Naylor, he's a tailor,
he makes trousers, suits and shirts.

2 Daisy Proctor, she's a doctor,
comes to see you when it hurts.

3 Francis Palmer, he's a farmer,
he's got cows and pigs and sheep.

4 Betty Witter, babysitter,
minds the kids when they're asleep.

5 Tina Meacher, language teacher,
teaches English, French and Greek.

6 Peter Gummer, he's a plumber,
call him when you've got a leak.

7 Debbie Prentice, she's a dentist,
keeps your teeth both clean and white.

8 Freddy Ryman, he's a fireman,
comes when there's a fire to fight.

Chorus People work in the country,
people work in the town.
people work day and night
to make the world go round. *(2x)*

L macht Bewegungen zum Liedtext, S hören das Lied und machen mit · S lesen Text mit und singen dazu · **D↑** S singen auswendig

AB S. 14
Flashcards

Look around: Police all over the world

CD 32 **1 Listen and point.**

What does a German policeman look like?

Texas, USA

London, Great Britain

Spain

North Korea

France

New York, USA

Italy

In case of emergency call 112 – all over Europe!

Einen Eindruck von Polizeiuniformen und -aufgaben in anderen Ländern bekommen · Informationen dazu auf Englisch verstehen · Unterschiede und Gemeinsamkeiten zur deutschen Polizei feststellen

AB S. 15

Clever Jack: Present a poster

Find information. | Make a poster. | Present.

1 Look and read.

2 Talk to a partner: *What's different?*

3 Make a poster.

A job for Leo

CD 33 **1 Listen and read.**

Geschichte hören und mitlesen · Fragen zur Geschichte beantworten ·
D⬆ Inhalt der Geschichte auf Englisch wiedergeben

Copy 21/22

Jobs in the classroom

CD 34 **1 Listen and read.**

2 Talk about jobs in your classroom.

3 D⬆ Write a job list for your class.

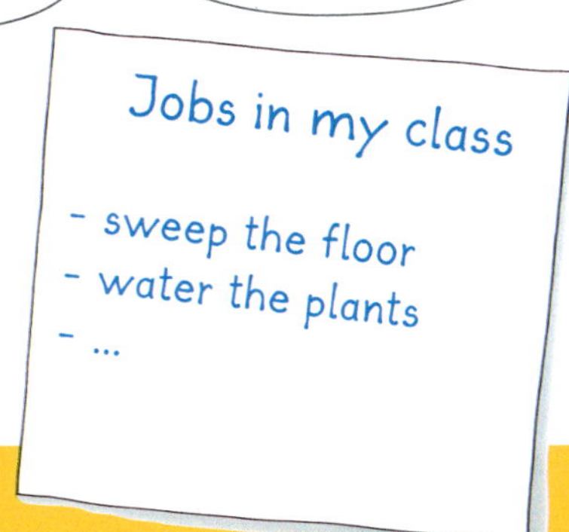

Clean your classroom

1 Play the game.

Spiel spielen, dabei Anzahl der gesetzten Felder mitzählen und Aktion auf erreichtem Feld ausführen: Piktogramm - Dienst auf Englisch benennen; Text - Dienst vorlesen und pantomimisch ausführen

Discovery tour

Can you find it?

Tongue twister

How many cookies
could a good cook cook
if a good cook
could cook cookies?

CD 37

What's the difference?

policeman	policemen
policewoman	policewomen

a.m. – p.m.

from 0.00 – 12.00 = a.m.

from 12.00 – 0.00 = p.m.

12.00 = noon

00.00 = midnight

I like to clean the blackboard. Which job in the classroom do you like best?

Green Day at school

Today is "Green Day" at Lucy's school.
"Green Day" is a project about
protecting nature.

At Lucy's school there's a "Green Day"
every month.
Some pupils are making recycled paper,
some pupils are collecting rubbish,
and some pupils are planting flowers
and a tree.
There are many things to do
to help nature.
"Green Day" is a fun day.

Do you have a "Green Day"
at your school?

CD 41 **1 Listen and point.**

2 Talk to a partner:
What do you do
to protect nature?
– I collect rubbish. And I …

3 Read the text.

Kinder anregen, ihr Wissen zum Thema einzubringen · Bildbeschreibung hören und auf Bildausschnitte zeigen · Einzelheiten des Bildes benennen/beschreiben · Fragen zum Bild beantworten · Dialog zum Umweltschutz führen · Text lesen · D ⬆ Text vorlesen

Planet Earth

CD 42 **1 Listen and read along.**

CD 43 **2 Listen and point.**

We live on Planet Earth.
It's a wonderful place to live.
And there's so much to explore!

See the water running in the rivers.

Hear the birds singing in the forest.

Planet Earth – a great place for all of us!

Look at all the animals in the fields.

Feel the sand on the beach.

3 Talk to a partner: *What's your favourite place on Earth?*
– My favourite place is …

Hörtext hören und auf passende Fotos zeigen · Text hören und lesen · **D** ⬆ Text vorlesen · sich über die schönsten Plätze auf der Erde austauschen · **D** ⬆ eine Collage erstellen

AB S. 20
Copy 23–25
Flashcards

Let's save the planet

1 **Read the poster.**

2 **Discuss with your friends:**
What can we do? – We can …

3 **D⬆ Make a poster for your classroom.**

Let's save the planet

- Collect glass, plastic, paper and cans.
- Reuse paper – each sheet has got two sides.
- Share your toys with your friends.
- Collect your batteries.
- Reuse plastic bags.
- Shut the door to keep the room warm.
- Switch off the lights when you leave the room.
- Walk to school, go by bike or take the bus.

Sätze lesen und mit eigenen Ergebnissen vergleichen · *Placemat*-Methode als Grundlage zur Diskussion über das Thema *Let's save the planet* anwenden · **D⬆** Poster für die Klasse erstellen

AB S. 21
Copy 26

Share your toys

CD 45 **1 Listen and read.**

Geschichte hören und mitlesen · Fragen zur Geschichte beantworten ·
D⬆ Inhalt der Geschichte auf Englisch wiedergeben

Rubbish rap

CD 46
CD 47

1 Listen and read along.

2 Say the rap.

Reduce, recycle, reuse (3x)

This is our planet
We've only got this one
To keep it in good shape
Something must be done.

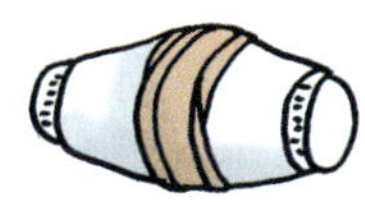

Reduce, recycle, reuse (3x)

We all can help our planet
It's up to you and me
We have to change our habits
Let's start right now, you'll see.

Reduce, recycle, reuse (3x)

Reduce your waste and rubbish
Recycle what you can
Reuse your toys and clothes –
Become a Green Day fan.

Reduce, recycle, reuse (4 x)

ZOOM IN

Recycling paper

CD 48 **1 Listen and read.**

2 Read and explain the paper cycle.

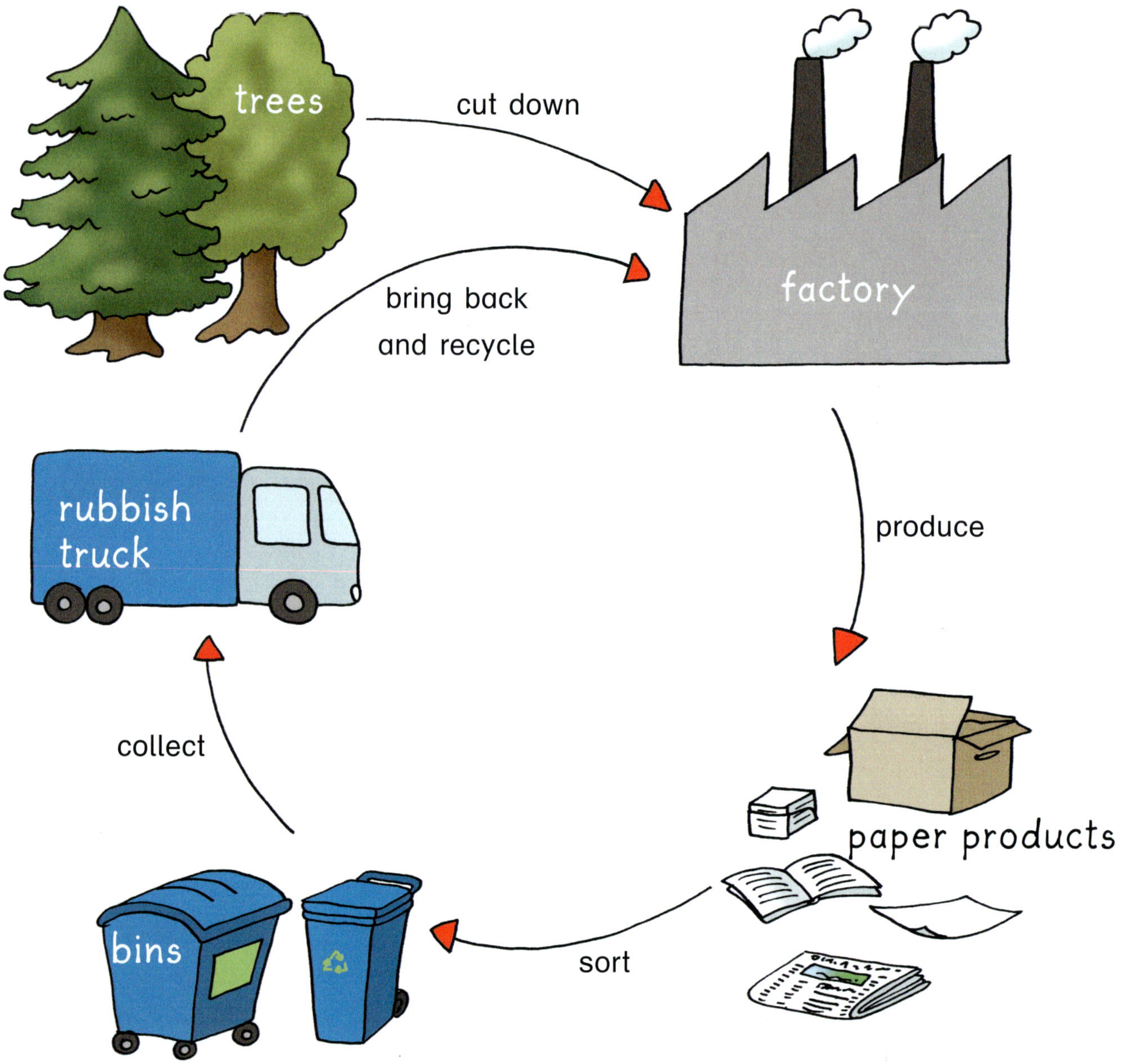

3 Talk to a partner: *What is made of paper?*

– … is/are made of paper.

Sich über den Papierkreislauf informieren · ein Schaubild lesen und darüber sprechen · mit einem Partner sammeln, was aus Papier hergestellt wird · **D ⬆** Wörter/Sätze aufschreiben

AB S. 23
Copy 30

Reusing paper

1 Read and do.

Paper cup

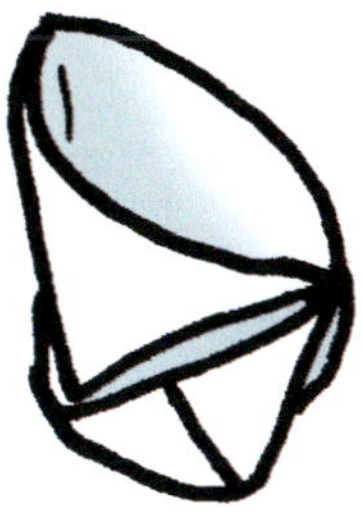

1 Fold your square in half diagonally.

2 Place it with the folded edge towards you.

3 Fold one corner to the center of the opposite side.

4 Fold the other corner in the same way.

5 Fold the top flaps down to make a cup.

Paper beads

1 Cut long triangles out of magazines.

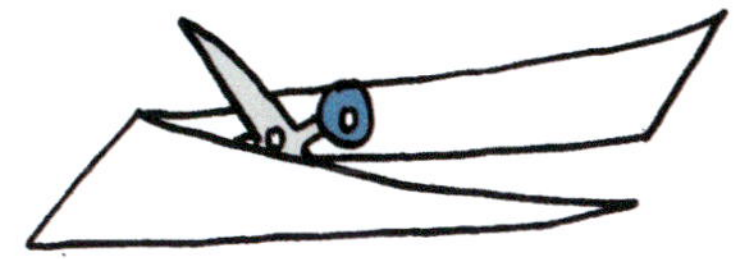

2 Put a little bit of glue on the pointed end.

3 Roll the triangle around a toothpick. Start at the wide end and roll tightly.

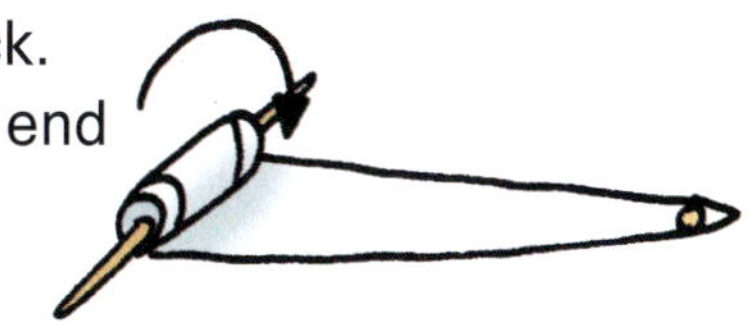

4 Finish the rolling and glue the tip of the triangle to the rolled paper. Hold it for a moment to stick together.

5 Remove your bead and let it dry.

Bastelanleitungen lesen und Becher bzw. Perlen entsprechend herstellen ·
D ↑ weitere Bastelanleitungen überlegen, bei denen Altpapier genutzt wird

AB S. 26

Time for a poem

CD 51
CD 52

1 Listen and read along.

Trees
are good
for you and me.
They are important
for all of us – let's make sure
we keep the trees alive.
We need them,
they need us.
stem stem stem
root root root root root root

2 Say the poem and act it out.

The chestnut
Small, brown, and round
a chestnut falls to the ground.
Down comes the rain
and the chestnut grows again.
Out comes the sun –
watch the chestnut grow, it's fun!
Some years later – come and see,
a big and wonderful chestnut tree.

Gedichte hören und (mit)lesen · *The chestnut* mit Bewegungen begleiten ·
D ⬆ ein eigenes Gedicht schreiben

AB S. 24, 25

Discovery tour

Can you find it?

The daily use of paper

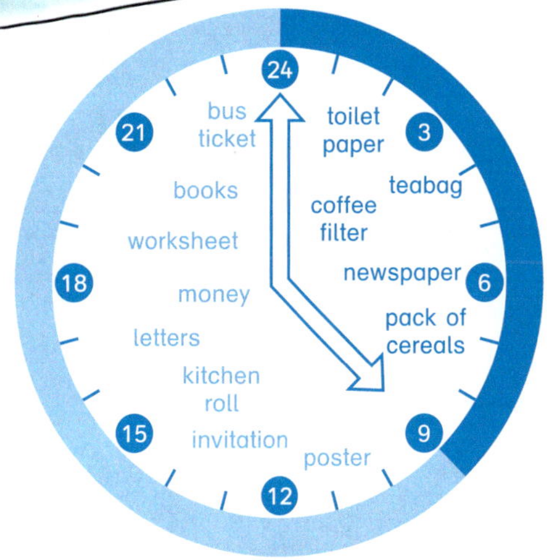

Did you know that …

… in Germany each person uses about 65 plastic bags each year?

… the average German uses 236 kg of paper per year? That is 640 g per day – one book about *Harry Potter*!

… each person in Germany uses about 120 litres of drinking water per day? We use it for brushing our teeth, cooking, washing our clothes, flushing the toilet, …

Rubbish bins in Namibia

Bildausschnitte im Kapitel finden und über die Seite sprechen · täglichen Papierverbrauch bewusst machen und ggf. Beispiele ergänzen · über Möglichkeiten sprechen, wie man Müll trennen kann · Fakten zur Umwelteinwirkung durch den Menschen kennenlernen und ggf. Beispiele ergänzen

AB S. 27
Portfolio (Copy)

At the zoo

Today Lucy, her parents
and Jack are at the zoo.
It's a sunny day.
There are many people
at the zoo.
Look at all the animals:
the giraffes, the penguins,
the hippos and the monkeys.

Lucy and Jack are very excited.
They are looking at the lions.
Lucy's mother wants to see
the elephants.
She has got a zoo map in
her hands to find the way.
Dad's favourite animals are
the parrots.

What's your favourite zoo animal?

CD 56 **1 Listen and point.**

2 Talk to a partner:
What would you like to see?
– I'd like to see ...

3 Read the text.

Kinder anregen, ihr Wissen zum Thema einzubringen · Bildbeschreibung hören und auf Bildausschnitte zeigen · Einzelheiten des Bildes benennen/beschreiben · Fragen zum Bild beantworten, z.B. *How many ...? Where's ...?* · Dialog führen · Text lesen · **D⬆** Text vorlesen

AB S. 28
Copy 31/32
Flashcards
Poster

Animals at Blue Hill Zoo

CD 60 **1 Listen and point.**

1

2

3
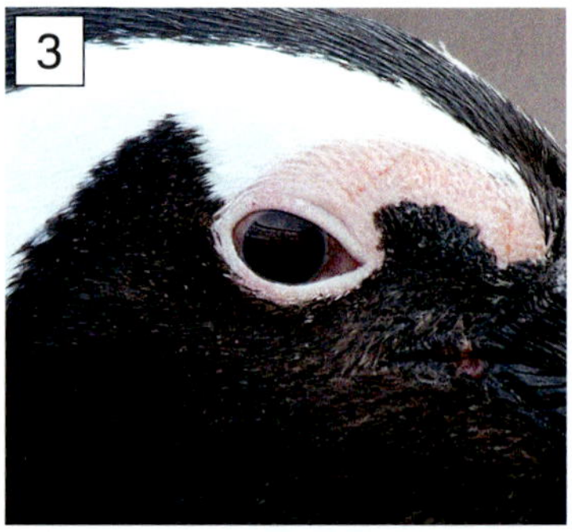
4

5

6

2 Read.

Dad: Where would you like to go?
Jack: Let's go to the monkeys.
Mum: I'd like to see the elephants.
Lucy: We must see the lions.
Dad: Okay.
Let's look at the map to find the way.

3 Play a game: *At the zoo I can see a monkey.*
– At the zoo I can see a monkey and a parrot.
– At the zoo I can see a monkey, a parrot and a …

Text hören und auf entsprechende Tiere zeigen · Dialog lesen und variieren · Wortschatzspiel durchführen · Lied *Going to the zoo* singen

AB S. 29, 30
Copy 36
CD 58/59

Watch out!

CD 61 **1 Listen and read.**

Clever Jack: Find keywords

Read. Find. Mark.

1 Read.

2 Look at the two texts and talk to a partner: *What's different?*

There are many different penguins.
Penguins live in Australia, New Zealand,
South America and South Africa.
Penguins like to eat fish.
They have got feathers like all birds.
Penguins lay eggs.
They have got wings – but they can't fly.

There are many different penguins.
Penguins live in Australia, New Zealand,
South America and South Africa.
Penguins like to eat fish.
They have got feathers like all birds.
Penguins lay eggs.
They have got wings – but they can't fly.

Lernstrategie bewusst machen: das Finden von Schlüsselwörtern erläutern ·
Texte lesen, auf unterschiedliche Lösungen (inhaltlich / Art der Markierung) aufmerksam werden und sich darüber austauschen

AB S. 31

Lions in the wild

CD 64 **1 Listen and read.**

Lions are very big cats.
They live in Africa, in the savannah.
Lions are very social.
They live in groups called prides.
There can be up to 30 lions in a pride.
Lions can live for 10 to 14 years.

Lions are strong animals that can run very fast. They have got big teeth and a long tail. Male lions have got a mane.

Female lions have 2 to 3 cubs at a time.
Lions hunt in groups, for example zebras, antelopes and other large animals. They usually hunt at night.
Did you know that lions rest for around 20 hours a day?

2 D⬆ Write your own text.

CD 62
CD 63 **3 Sing the song.** ♪♩𝅗𝅥

Text hören und Schlüsselwörter erkennen · Text hören und mitlesen · **D⬆** eigenen Text verfassen · Lied *The lion sleeps tonight* singen

AB S. 32, 33
Copy 33, 38 – 41

The lion and the mouse

CD 65 ## 1 Listen and read.

A big lion was sleeping under a tree.

Suddenly a little mouse ran over his shoulder.

The lion woke up and grabbed the mouse.

"I'm going to eat you!" he shouted.

"Please, don't eat me," said the mouse. "Maybe I can help you one day."

The lion laughed. "That's funny! Okay, mouse – run!" he said.

Geschichte hören und mitlesen · Fragen zur Geschichte beantworten · Geschichte mit verteilten Rollen vorlesen

Storycards

Three weeks later,
two hunters caught the lion.

They tied him to a tree.
The lion roared, but he couldn't get free.

The mouse heard the lion
and ran to him.

She quickly bit through the rope.

The lion was free.

In the zoo shop

CD 67 **1 Listen and point.**

2 Talk to a partner: *What would you like to buy?*
– I'd like to buy ...

Lucy: Good morning!
Mr Tims: Hello. Can I help you?
Lucy: Yes please, I'd like to buy three postcards.
Have you got postcards?
Mr Tims: Yes, of course we have. Here you are.
Lucy: Thank you.
Mr Tims: Anything else?
Lucy: No, thanks. How much are the postcards?
Mr Tims: £ 2.10, please.
Lucy: Here you are. And thank you for your help.
Mr Tims: You're welcome. Bye.
Lucy: Bye-bye.

3 Read the dialogue. **4 D⬆ Act out the dialogue.**

Hörverstehen durch Zeigen auf Bildausschnitte deutlich machen · sich über eigene Kaufwünsche mit einem Partner austauschen *What would you like to buy? – I'd like to buy ...* · Dialog lesen · D⬆ Rollenspiel zur Kaufsituation einüben und präsentieren

AB S. 34
Copy 44 /45

Discovery tour

Can you find it?

Animal riddle

My animal is black and white.
It has got two legs and feathers.
It can swim but it can't fly.

CD 70

What is it?

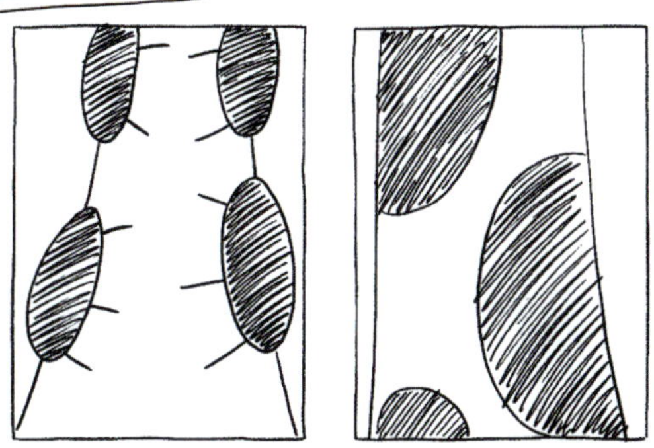

do not – don't

If I were an animal
I would be a monkey.
And you?

Bildausschnitte im Kapitel finden und über die Seite sprechen · Tierrätsel hören und lösen · eigene Tierrätsel ausdenken · Witz verstehen · *Language awareness*: auf *do not / don't* aufmerksam werden · eigenen Wunsch äußern

CD 70
AB S. 35
Portfolio (Copy)

Around the world

Andrew and his family are at the airport. They are moving to New York because Andrew's father has got a new job there.

Lucy and her friends are saying goodbye.
They have got a present for Andrew.

The airport is very big.
Here you can meet people from many different countries.
You can fly around the world from here.
You can go to the USA, Canada, India, Germany, Australia or South Africa.

Have you been to the airport?

CD 74 **1 Listen and point.**

2 Talk to a partner:
Where would you like to go? – I'd like to go to … because …

3 Read the text.

Friends

CD 75 **1 Listen and read.**

Geschichte hören und mitlesen · Fragen zur Geschichte beantworten · D ⬆ Inhalt der Geschichte auf Englisch wiedergeben

Copy 46/47

The friendship book

CD 76 **1 Listen and read.**

What do you like?

What's your favourite subject?

What is your favourite colour?

My name: Lucy

My favourite colour is blue.

My favourite animal is my lion Leo.

My favourite food is fish and chips.

My favourite subject is music.

When I grow up I want to be a singer or a policewoman.

I like sunshine, laughing, swimming, singing and eating chocolate.

My wish for you: Have lots of fun in the USA. Don't forget us, Andrew.

My name: Jack

My favourite colour is green.

My favourite animal is a rabbit.

My favourite food is apple pie.

My favourite subject is maths.

When I grow up I want to be a pilot.

I like football, in-line skating and playing with my friends.

My wish for you: I hope you will find a new friend in America.

Come back soon!

What do you want to be?

What is your favourite food?

What's your favourite animal?

2 Work with a partner. Answer the questions. ...

Look around: We speak English

CD 79 **1 Listen and read.**

Felix is from Germany.
He *learns* English at school.

Sabita is from India.
She *learns* English at school.

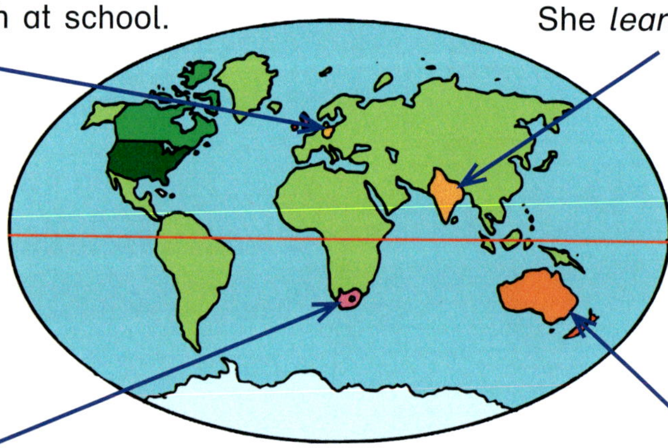

Sonwabile is from South Africa.
She *learns* English at school.

John is from Australia.
He *speaks* English at home.

2 Talk to a partner:

I speak … at home.
I learn … at school.

3 D⬆ Name countries where children learn English at school.

Informationen zu den Kindern verstehen und mitlesen · sich mit einem Partner über die eigenen Sprachen austauschen · D⬆ Länder nennen, in denen Englisch gesprochen wird

AB S. 39/40
Copy 48/49

News from Andrew

CD 83 **1 Listen and read.**

2 Work with a partner: *There is a …/There are …/ On this picture I can see …*

3 D⬆ Read the text out loud.

http://Andrew-in-New-York.blog/ search...

Andrew's blog

May 28th – 14.26

The friendship book is wonderful.

I miss you! 

Life in New York is very exciting.
I see something new every day.

I have got a new friend. His name is Carlos. He is also 10 years old. Carlos and I play basketball together. He is very funny. We laugh a lot.

Last week we read a story about a girl called Sacagawea. Here's the story for you. Do you like it?

What's new in Windsor?

Sacagawea and the rattlesnake

CD 85 **1 Listen and read.**

2 D⬆ Tell the story in your own words.

Geschichte hören • Verstehen durch Zeigen auf entsprechende Bilder deutlich machen • Fragen zur Geschichte beantworten • Geschichte mit verteilten Rollen vorlesen • D↑ Geschichte nacherzählen

AB S. 42
Copy 52/53
Storycards

ZOOM IN The American flag

1 Look at the flags and count the stars.

How many?

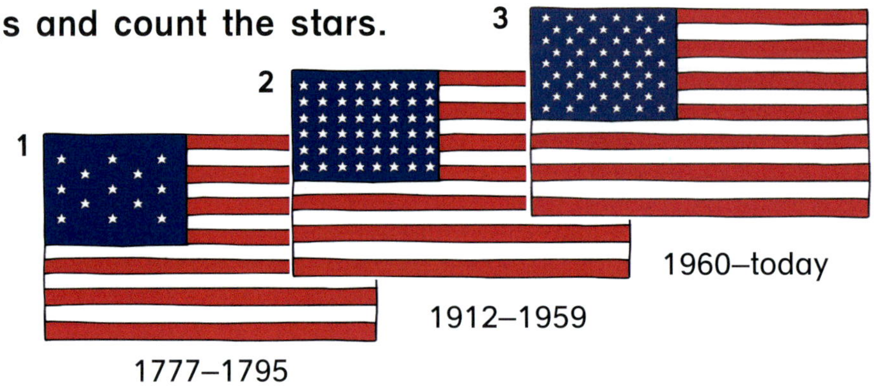

2 Read the text.

Do you know the American flag
has changed over the years?
Today it has got 50 stars
and 13 stripes:
one star for each state,
one stripe for each colony.
When the flag is on
the White House,
the president is at home.

3 Listen.

CD 86

I pledge allegiance to the flag ...

Text lesen · Sterne (und Streifen) zählen · *Intercultural awareness:*
Etwas über die amerikanische Geschichte und die amerikanische Flagge erfahren

Discovery tour

CD 87

The only way to have a friend is to be one.
Ralph Waldo Emerson

Fit for class 5

1 Read.

2 Act out the dialogues.

This is Lucy. Lucy **is** 10 years old.

This is Leo. Leo **is** a lion.

This is Jack. Jack **is** Lucy's best friend.

These are Emma, Ben, David and Matilda.

They **are** Lucy's friends.

Emma **has got** a tortoise.

Ben **has got** a goldfish.

Lucy **has got** Leo.

Lucy **likes** music.

Jack **doesn't** like swimming.

Kinder verschaffen sich einen Überblick über eine Auswahl der gelernten sprachlichen Strukturen • Kinder lesen in Partner- bzw. Gruppenarbeit die Dialoge und übertragen die Inhalte im Gespräch auf eigene Situation

boy — boys

girl — girls

child — children

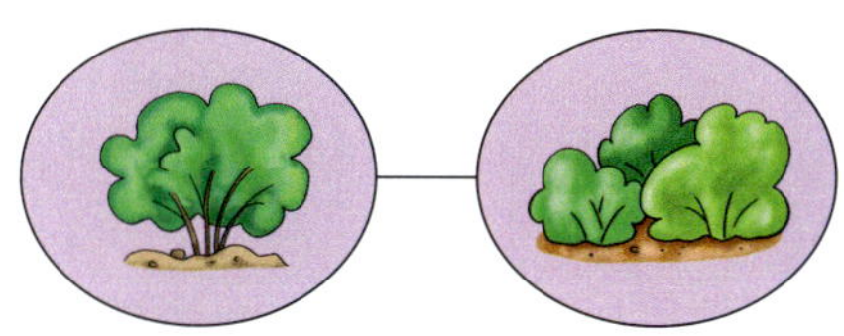

bush — bushes

How many tennis balls can you see?
How many children are in the picture on the left?
How many chairs can you see?

There are seven tennis balls.
I can see eight children.
There are four boys and four girls.
There is one chair.

Halloween

CD 92 **1 Listen and read.**

CD 93 **2 Say the rhyme.**

What do you know about Halloween?

Halloween is a very old festival.
It comes from Ireland.
It is on October 31st.

Today children have parties on that day.
They dress up as witches and ghosts.
They go from house to house
and ask for treats.

Trick or treat,
trick or treat,
give us something nice to eat.

Nuts and candy,
fruit and gum,
we'll go away
if you give us some.

Kinder anregen, ihr Wissen zum Thema einzubringen • Text hören und mitlesen • Einzelheiten des Bildes benennen/beschreiben • Fragen zum Bild beantworten, z. B. *Where's ...? / Can you find ?* / *How many ... can you see?* • Reim hören • **D** ⬆ Reim auswendig sprechen

AB S. 47
Copy 54 – 56

Festivals of light

CD 96  **1 Listen and read along.**

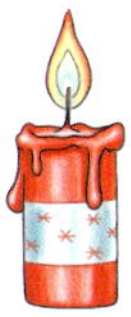

All over the world people use candles when they celebrate.
When it gets dark in autumn and winter
you can find many different festivals of light.

Sankta Lucia – Santa Lucia

People in Sweden and Sicily celebrate this festival on 13th December. The girls are wearing white dresses and one of them is wearing a ring with seven candles on her head.

Diwali

Diwali takes place in India.
The festival lasts for five days. People put up many oil lamps to celebrate the victory of the good over the bad.

Hanukkah

Hanukkah is a Jewish festival.
It takes place in December.
It lasts for eight days.
On the last day the whole family gets together. They have a big meal and give each other presents.

Christmas

Christian people celebrate Christmas on the 24th and the 25th December to remember Jesus' birthday.
It's a family party and people give each other presents.

Word list

A

a/an ein/eine
airport der Flughafen
alive lebendig
always immer
a.m. vormittags
and und
angel der Engel
angry ärgerlich
animal das Tier
ant die Ameise
around um, herum
(to) ask fragen
autumn der Herbst

B

babysitter der Babysitter
bakery die Bäckerei
bat die Fledermaus
battery Batterie
(to) be sein
beach der Strand
bee die Biene
behind hinter
bell die Glocke
between zwischen
big groß
bike das Fahrrad
bin der Mülleimer/- korb
bird der Vogel
black schwarz
blackbird die Amsel
blue blau
body der Körper
book das Buch
bottle die Flasche
box die Schachtel
branch der Ast
brave mutig
broom der Besen
brown braun
bus driver der Busfahrer, die Busfahrerin
bus (stop) der Bus, (die Bushaltestelle)
bush der Busch
butterfly der Schmetterling
(to) buy kaufen

C

can (can't) können, (nicht können)
candle die Kerze
capital die Hauptstadt
car das Auto
castle das Schloss
cat die Katze
cauldron der Kessel
(to) celebrate feiern
(to) change wechseln
(to) check prüfen
chestnut die Kastanie
chocolate bar der Schokoriegel
Christmas Day der erste Weihnachtstag
Christmas Eve Heiligabend
church die Kirche
cinema das Kino
(to) circle einkreisen
city die Innen-/Großstadt
(to) clean the blackboard die Tafel wischen
(to) climb klettern
(to) come kommen
comic der Comic
(to) collect sammeln
(to) colour anmalen
cook der Koch
country Land
cracker der Knallbonbon
crisps die Chips
crocodile das Krokodil
(to) cut down reduzieren

D

day der Tag
dentist der Zahnarzt
(to) do machen
doctor der Arzt, die Ärztin
(to) draw zeichnen
duck die Ente

E

egg(s) das Ei, die Eier
elephant der Elefant

English Englisch
envelope der Umschlag
excited aufgeregt
(to) explore entdecken
eye das Auge

F

face das Gesicht
factory die Fabrik
farmer der Landwirt
favourite Lieblings-
feather die Feder
(to) feed füttern
festival das Fest
(to) fill in ausfüllen
fine gut, fein
fireman der Feuerwehrmann
flag die Fahne
flight der Flug
flower die Blume
(to) flush the toilet spülen
(to) fly fliegen
folder der Schnellhefter
foot (feet) der Fuß (die Füße)
football player der Fußballspieler
forest der Wald
fox der Fuchs
France Frankreich
friendship book das Freundschaftsalbum
fun der Spaß

G

German Deutsch
Germany Deutschland
ghost das Gespenst
giraffe die Giraffe
(to) give geben
(to) give away weggeben
glass das Glas
(to) go by ... mit dem ... fahren
(to) go straight on geradeaus gehen
grass das Gras
Great Britain Großbritannien
green grün
ground der Boden
(to) grow wachsen

H

habit die Gewohnheit
hand die Hand
handwriting die Handschrift
happy glücklich
has (got) hat
hat der Hut
(to) have got haben
he er
head der Kopf
headline die Überschrift
hedgehog der Igel
hippo das Flusspferd
his/her sein/ihr
holidays die Ferien, der Urlaub
hospital das Krankenhaus
(to) hunt jagen

I

I ich
ice cream das Eis
in in
in front of vor
invitation die Einladung
(to) invite einladen
it es
Italy Italien

J

job der Beruf
(to) jump springen

K

(to) keep behalten

L

ladybird der Marienkäfer
lake der See
lamp die Lampe
leg das Bein
light das Licht
(to) light leuchten
(to) like mögen

lion der Löwe
(to) listen to (zu)hören
(to) live leben

M

(to) make machen
many viele
map die Karte, der Plan
mechanic der Mechaniker, die Mechanikerin
mistletoe der Mistelzweig
mole der Maulwurf
monkey der Affe
mountain der Berg
mouse die Maus
my mein, meine

N

nature die Natur
(to) need benötigen, brauchen
nest das Nest
never nie
new neu
newspaper die Zeitung
next to neben
(to) nod nicken
nurse die Kranken-schwester, der Krankenpfleger

O

ocean das Meer
old alt
on auf
open offen
orange orange
our unser
owl die Eule

P

paper (product) das Papier(produkt)
park der Park
parrot der Papagei
(to) pass reichen, geben
pear die Birne
pearl die Perle
pencil der Bleistift
penguin der Pinguin
picture das Bild
pilot der Pilot
pink pink, lila
planet Earth der Planet Erde
(to) plant pflanzen
plastic das Plastik
(to) play spielen
playground der Spielplatz
plumber der Klempner
p.m. nachmittags
(to) point zeigen
policeman, policewoman der Polizist, die Polizistin
postcard die Postkarte
poster das Poster
postman der Briefträger
present das Geschenk
(to) present präsentieren
(to) produce produzieren
(to) protect schützen
proud stolz
pumpkin der Kürbis
pupil der Schüler, die Schülerin

Qu

R

rabbit das Kaninchen
rattlesnake die Klapperschlange
(to) read lesen
(to) recycle aufbereiten
recycling das Recycling
recycling bin die Wertstofftonne
red rot
(to) reduce reduzieren
(to) remember sich erinnern
rest der Rest
(to) reuse wiederverwenden
rice der Reis
riddle das Rätsel
river der Fluss
robin das Rotkehlchen
rubbish der Müll

(to) run rennen

S

sad traurig
Santa Claus der Weihnachtsmann
(to) save sparen
(to) say sagen
scared verängstigt
seal der Seehund
(to) shake schütteln
shape die Form
she sie
shell die Muschel
shop assistant der Verkäufer, die Verkäuferin
(to) shut (the door) (die Tür) schließen
(to) sit sitzen
skin die Haut
snack box die Brotdose
snake die Schlange
soft drink die Limonade
someone jemand
something etwas
sometimes manchmal
(to) speak sprechen
spider die Spinne
squirrel das Eichhörnchen
star der Stern
station der Bahnhof
stocking der Weihnachtssocken
stone der Stein
story die Geschichte
(to) sweep the floor den Fußboden fegen
(to) swim schwimmen
(to) switch off ausschalten

T

tail der Schwanz
tailor der Schneider
(to) take out the rubbish den Müll rausbringen
(to) talk reden
teacher der Lehrer, die Lehrerin
the der, die, das
(to) tick abhaken
ticket die Eintrittskarte, die Fahrkarte
(to) tidy up säubern, putzen
tiger der Tiger
tired müde
toilet paper das Toilettenpapier
tooth (teeth) der Zahn, (die Zähne)
(to) touch berühren
town die Stadt
town hall das Rathaus
toy(s) das (die) Spielzeug(e)
tree der Baum
(to) turn right/left rechts/links abbiegen
twig der Zweig

U

under unter

V

vegetables das Gemüse
vet der Tierarzt, die Tierärztin

W

(to) walk zu Fuß gehen
water das Wasser
waterfall der Wasserfall
(to) water (the plants) (die Pflanzen) gießen
weather das Wetter
weekend das Wochenende
white weiß
wing der Flügel
witch die Hexe
word das Wort
(to) work arbeiten
world die Welt

X

Y

yellow gelb

Z

zebra das Zebra

	Die Schülerinnen und Schüler ...	In town	People at work	Green Day at school	At the zoo	Around the world
Hör-/Hör-Seh-Verstehen	... verstehen didaktisierte und authentische fiktionale Texte und entnehmen ihnen zentrale Informationen.	PB S. 4, PB S. 5, PB S. 7, PB S. 8, PB S. 9, PB S. 10, PB S. 11 AB S. 5, AB S. 8, AB S. 11	PB S. 15, PB S. 16, PB S. 20, PB S. 21 AB S. 12, AB S. 15, AB S. 17, AB S. 19	PB S. 25, PB S. 26, PB S. 28, PB S. 32 AB S. 24, AB S. 27	PB S. 35, PB S. 37, PB S. 40, PB S. 41, PB S. 42 AB S. 34, AB S. 35	PB S. 45, PB S. 46, , PB S. 47, PB S. 49, PB S. 50, PB S. 51 AB S. 39, AB S. 40, AB S. 41, AB S. 43
	... verstehen kindgemäße Sachtexte und entnehmen ihnen relevante Aussagen.	PB S. 6, PB S. 12	PB S. 18 AB S. 18	PB S. 30, PB S. 31	PB S. 39 AB S. 28, AB S. 32	PB S. 48 AB S. 38
Sprechen	... beteiligen sich verbal am Unterrichtsgeschehen.	PB S. 5, PB S. 12 AB S. 5	PB S. 19, PB S. 21	PB S. 27, PB S. 31, PB S. 32 AB S. 23, AB S. 24	PB S. 36, PB S. 38, PB S. 40, PB S. 41, PB S. 42 AB S. 29, AB S. 31, AB 33	PB S. 50, PB S. 51, PB S. 52 AB S. 36, AB 37, AB 38, AB S. 44
	... gebrauchen vertraute formelhafte Wendungen und Sätze, um Personen, Dinge und Handlungen zu beschreiben.	PB S. 5, PB S. 6, PB S. 7, PB S. 8, PB S. 10, PB S. 12 AB S. 5, AB S. 7	PB S. 15, PB S. 16, PB S. 19, PB S. 20, PB S. 21, PB S. 23 AB S. 15, AB S. 17	PB S. 25, PB S. 26, PB S. 27, PB S. 28, PB S. 30, PB S. 33 AB S. 24, AB S. 25	PB S. 35, PB S. 37, PB S. 43 AB S. 31	PB S. 45, PB S. 46, PB S. 47, PB S. 48, PB S. 49, PB S. 50/51, PB S. 53 AB S. 37, AB S. 38, AB S. 39
	... erzählen und berichten in vertrauten Wendungen und Sätzen über Ereignisse bzw. Erlebnisse.	PB S. 5, PB S. 9, PB S. 12	PB S. 15, PB S. 18	PB S. 25, , PB S. 26, PB S. 33	PB S. 35, PB S. 43	PB S. 45, PB S. 53

Lesen	... verstehen schriftliche Aussagen und kurze Erklärungen auf Satzebene in einem bekannten Kontext.	PB S. 7, PB S. 12, PB S. 13 AB S. 4, AB S. 5, AB S. 7	PB S. 18, PB S. 19, PB S. 23 AB S. 13, AB S. 16, AB S. 19	PB S. 26, PB S. 27, PB S. 31, PB S. 33 AB S. 21, AB S. 22	PB S. 43 AB S. 28, AB S. 30	PB S. 47, PB S. 48, PB S. 52, PB S. 53 AB S. 36, AB S. 38, AB S. 41
	... verstehen kurze (auch authentische) Texte mit bekanntem Wortschatz und entnehmen die wesentlichen Handlungselemente.	PB S. 5, PB S. 8, PB S. 9, PB S. 11 AB S. 8	PB S. 15, PB S. 17, PB S. 20 AB S. 18	PB S. 25, PB S. 28, PB S. 29, PB S. 32, PB S. 33 AB S. 24, AB S. 26	PB S. 35, PB S. 37, PB S. 38, PB S. 39, PB S. 40, PB S. 41 AB S. 29, AB S. 31. AB S. 32, AB S. 34	PB S. 45, PB S. 46, PB S. 49, PB S. 50, PB S. 51 AB S. 42, AB S. 46
	... entnehmen kommunikativen Kurztexten wesentliche Informationen.	PB S. 7, PB S. 13	PB S. 16, PB S. 21. PB S. 23, PB S. 20	PB S. 28	PB S. 36, PB S. 37, PB S. 42, PB S. 43	PB S. 46, PB S. 47, PB S. 53 AB S. 38
Schreiben	... beschriften Bilder mithilfe von bekanntem oder im Wörterbuch gefundenem Wortmaterial.	AB S. 6, AB S. 7, AB S. 9	AB S. 14	AB S. 22, AB S. 24	AB S. 28	AB S. 42
	... lösen bzw. erstellen einfache Rätsel mithilfe von bekanntem oder im Bildwörterbuch gefundenem Wortmaterial.	AB S. 4, AB S. 5, AB S. 6, AB S. 7, AB S. 9	AB S. 12	AB S. 20	AB S. 31	AB S. 36, AB S. 38, AB S. 39
	... verfassen kurze Texte durch das Zusammenfügen von Satzelementen oder Textbausteinen.	AB S. 4, AB S. 10, AB S. 11	PB S. 19 AB S. 13, AB S. 15, AB S. 18, AB S. 19	PB S. 27, PB S. 30, PB S. 32 AB S. 20, AB S. 21, AB S. 25, AB S. 26, AB S. 27	PB S. 39 AB S. 29, AB S. 30, AB S. 32, AB S. 35	AB S. 36, AB S. 37, AB S. 41, AB S. 43
Sprachmittlung	... geben Einzelheiten von Gelesenem auf Deutsch wieder.	PB S. 8, PB S. 9	PB S. 20	PB S. 28	PB S. 37	PB S. 46
	... erklären global verstandenes Gelesenes auf Deutsch.	PB S. 8, PB S. 9	PB S. 20	PB S. 28, PB S. 33	PB S. 37	PB S. 46

Discovery 4 auf der Grundlage von:

Discovery 1 – 4 und Discovery 3 – 4 erarbeitet von Melanie Behrendt, Grit Bergner, Barbara Christmann, Karen B. Finck, Nadine Gulden, Kirstin Jebautzke, Nikola Mayer, Ute Schwickert, Astrid Stelter

Bildquellennachweis

|Alamy Stock Photo (RMB), Abingdon/Oxfordshire: Beaver, Vicki 18.1; Doyle, Paul 18.6; Eveleigh, Mark 18.2; JLImages 52.1; Maskot 57.1; Segre, Alex 12.4; Titmuss, Peter 16.2. |Bergner, Dr. Grit, Stadtroda: 41.1. |dreamstime.com, Brentwood: Pascalinaclaudiu 18.7. |fotolia.com, New York: chbaum 36.6; Meewezen, Manuel 36.4; Oosthuizen, Alta 36.3; Rivero, Eduardo 36.5; Schuler, Jan 36.2. |Getty Images, München: 2013 Geovien So 18.4; Gamma-Rapho 18.5; Simpson, Stephen 52.3. |Glow Images GmbH c/o Regus, München: 12.6; Michael Weber 12.2; SuperStock 12.3. |Interfoto, München: Delimont, Danita/Jannsen, Brian 18.3. |iStockphoto.com, Calgary: asiseeit 16.5; ilbusca 12.5; MiguelMalo 16.6; ollo 16.1; Schmidt, Chris 12.1; skodonnell 57.4; yogesh_more 57.2. |Jebautzke, Kirstin, Braunschweig: 33.2. |Krause, Ute, Windhoek: 39.1, 39.2. |laif, Köln: Jonkmanns, Bernd 49.1, 49.2. |OKAPIA KG - Michael Grzimek & Co., Frankfurt/M.: OSF/Rosing, Norbert 39.3. |PantherMedia GmbH (panthermedia.net), München: 36.1; Trautmann, Arne 16.4. |Shutterstock.com, New York: Africa Studio 57.3; Andrushko, Galyna 26.1; Baronb 26.4, 33.1; bikeriderlondon 16.3; Krzeslak, Piotr 26.3; Novikov, Sergey 26.2; Thaiview 26.5. |Thinkstock, Sandyford/Dublin: Getty Images/Big Cheese Photo 52.2.